Tough Topics

Fighting

Elizabeth Raum

Heinemann Library
Chicago, Illinois

© 2008 Heinemann Library
a division of Reed Elsevier Inc.
Chicago, Illinois

Customer Service 888-454-2279

Visit our website at www.heinemannlibrary.com

Designed by Joanna Hinton-Malivoire
Photo research by Tracy Cummins and Tracey Engel
Printed in China by South China Printing.

12 11 10 09
10 9 8 7 6 5 4 3 2

Library of Congress Cataloging-in-Publication Data
Raum, Elizabeth.
  Fighting / Elizabeth Raum.
      p. cm. -- (Tough topics)
  Includes bibliographical references and index.
  ISBN-13: 978-1-4329-0819-5 (hc), ISBN-10: 1-4329-0819-7 (hc)
  ISBN-13: 978-1-4329-0824-9 (pb), ISBN-10: 1-4329-0824-3 (pb)
1. Fighting (Psychology)--Juvenile literature. I. Title.
  BF723.F5R38 2008
  303.6--dc22

                                        2007034030

Acknowledgments
The author and publisher are grateful to the following for permission to reproduce copyright material:
©age fotostock p. 10 (John Birdsall); ©Corbis pp. 9 (John Birdsall), 12 (Richard Hutchings), 17
(Randy Faris), 20, 22 (Tom Grill), 25 (zefa/Charles Gullung), 26 (zefa/Heide Benser), 27 (Little Blue
Wolf Productions/Royalty Free); ©Getty Images pp. 6 (NBAE/Warren Skalski), 7 (PhotoDisc/SW
Productions), 8 (Henrik Sorensen), 13 (Erin Patrice O'Brien), 16 (AFP/ATTILA KISBENEDEK), 18
(Peter Cade), 23 (Royalty Free), 24 (Ryuhei Shindo); ©Index Stock Imagery p. 15 (ThinkStock LLC);
©istockphoto pp. 4, 19, 28; ©Jupiter Images pp. 5 (Workbook Stock), 29 (Comstock Images); ©Photo
Researchers, Inc. p. 11 (Catherine Ursillo); ©Shutterstock p. 14 (Galina Barskaya).

Cover photograph reproduced with permission of ©Getty Images/Stockbyte.

The author would like to thank Ms. Helen Scully, Guidance Counselor, Central Elementary School,
Warren Township, New Jersey, for her valuable assistance.

Contents

Some words are shown in bold, **like this**. You can find out what they mean by looking in the Glossary.

Is This Fight Real?

Pow! When **superheroes** fight, we cheer. We want the superheroes to win the fight. Watching pretend fights in cartoons and movies can be fun.

▶Superheroes fight to save the world.

Some children pretend to fight like superheroes. In a pretend fight, no one gets hurt. No one is really angry.

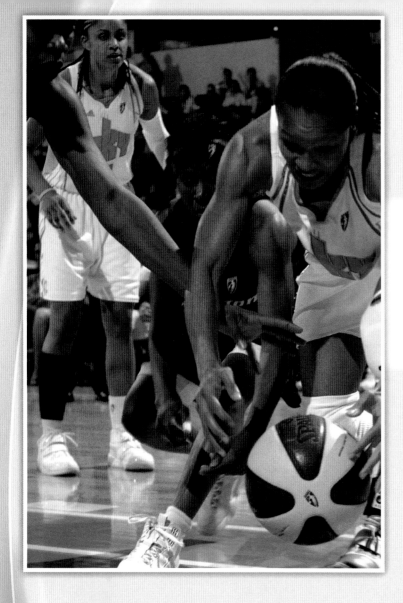

◄ These basketball players are fighting over the ball.

People use the word "fight" to mean many things. Soccer players, basketball players, or volleyball players may fight over the ball. This kind of fighting is part of the game.

But when fighting is real, it is not fun anymore. It is not play. Real fighting can be scary. Real fighting hurts everyone.

▲Someone may get hurt in a real fight.

Why Do People Fight?

Everyone **disagrees** sometimes. Brothers and sisters disagree. Friends disagree. Most of the time we can work out our problems.

▼Sometimes even best friends disagree.

▶Everyone feels like fighting sometimes.

But sometimes we get angry and refuse to give in. We are ready to fight for what we want or what we believe. For example, if we think something is unfair, we may yell and argue.

▲ People sometimes fight by shouting at each other.

Some people fight by yelling and screaming. They call each other names. They say hurtful things. This kind of fighting makes everyone feel bad.

Others fight by punching and kicking. They push and shove. This kind of fighting can cause bleeding and broken bones. It can cause hurt feelings, too.

▼Fighting never solves your problems.

◄ Some brothers and sisters fight when they disagree.

Fighting doesn't always mean people don't like each other. Sometimes it just means that they are tired or angry about something else in their lives. It may mean they want someone to listen to them.

But when people are fighting, they stop listening. Shouting doesn't solve problems. Neither does punching or hitting. There are better ways to work things out.

▲Some people fight by not talking.

What If I Feel Like Fighting?

Everyone gets angry. Remember that you are in charge of your own actions. Before you get into a fight, think about the choices you have.

▲Can these girls find a way to be friends again?

▲ Think before you speak.

It's okay to feel angry, but it's not okay to hurt someone. Stop before you say something hurtful. Stop before you start a fight.

▲ Fights begin when anger takes over.

It is hard to discuss a problem when you are angry. You need to calm down first. Step outside or into another room. Walk away.

When you leave, be sure to say, "I'll be back. We can talk later." It's important to let others know that you want to solve the problem. Try to calm down when you walk away.

▼Sometimes you need time by yourself.

◄Exercise might help you calm down.

If you are angry, take a deep breath and count to ten slowly. This will help you to calm down. Take time to do something you enjoy such as listening to music or playing outside.

When you are calm, talk to the person who made you angry. It's important to talk about the problem. Sometimes the other person doesn't know why you are upset. You must tell him or her.

◄ Tell others how you feel.

▲ These friends are talking using "feelings" messages.

Use "feelings" messages to explain how you are feeling. Be exact. Don't yell. Just tell the truth.

"Feelings" messages tell others what you feel. Try to say exactly how you feel so that the other person understands what made you angry. The next time you feel upset, use a "feelings" message to help you talk about how you feel.

To use a "feelings" message, tell someone:

When you _____,
(explain the action that made you feel upset)

I feel _____,
(explain how his or her action makes you feel)

and I wish _____.
(explain what actions would make you feel better)

▲ Take time to hear both sides.

You need to listen, too. Give others time to speak. Each person should have a chance to tell his or her side. It is fair to let each person explain how he or she is feeling.

▼These girls solved their problem by sharing.

Make a list of ways to solve the problem. Talk about taking turns, sharing, or other ways to get along. Together you can find a **solution**, a way to solve the problem.

▲ After you apologize, do something fun together.

If you hurt someone's feelings, break something belonging to someone else, or do something wrong, say you are sorry. It's not easy to **apologize**, but it's important. Saying you are sorry gives you a chance to start over again.

If someone apologizes to you, try to **forgive** him or her. A smile, a hug, a handshake, or a high-5 is a good way to say, "I forgive you." Working out a problem is difficult, but it is much better than fighting.

◄It feels good to forgive someone.

What If I See Others Fighting?

Watching or hearing other people fight can make you feel sad and scared. Someone might get hurt. You can help, but don't try to break up the fight.

▲ If you see a fight, stay out of the way.

▲Find an adult to help.

Don't just watch the fight either. Run and get help. Tell a parent, teacher, or police officer. Let an adult break up the fight.

Talk to an Adult

You can solve some problems, but others are too big. Talk to your parents if you or your friends have been fighting. Talk to them about what happened and how it made you feel. If you are worried or scared, your parents need to know.

◀ Parents can help.

▲Teachers can help, too.

Tell your teachers if you have a problem with fighting at school. They may have good ideas about how to stop children from hurting each other. They can help you solve the problem.

Glossary

apologize say you are sorry

apology words used to say you are sorry

disagree argue or have a different idea

forgive stop feeling angry or upset about something someone did

solution way to solve a problem

superhero make-believe person in cartoons, books, or movies who has special powers

Find Out More

Books to Read

Day, Roger. *Being Mad, Being Glad.* Chicago: Raintree, 2005.

Munson, Derek. *Enemy Pie.* San Francisco, CA: Chronicle Books, 2000.

Nelson, Robin. *Working With Others.* Minneapolis, MN: Lerner Publications, 2006.

Raatma, Lucia. *Peacefulness.* Mankato, MN: Bridgestone Books, 2000.

Websites

• TeachableMoment.org (http://www.teachablemoment.org/elementary/imessages.html) is a Website that explains how to use I-messages and avoid fighting.

• Nickelodeon.com (http://www.nick.com/all_nick/everything_nick/kaiser/violence_2.html) is a Website that contains helpful information about fighting.

Index